D0118732

GEORGE O'CONNOR

ATHENA

GREY-EYED GODDESS

A NEAL PORTER BOOK

New York & London

ALL OF US ARE BORN NAKED, HELPLESS, AND DEFENSELESS.

NOT SO PALLAS ATHENA.

MY SISTERS AND I ARE THE MOIRAE, ALSO KNOWN AS THE FATES. IT FALLS TO US TO SPIN, MEASURE, AND ULTIMATELY SEVER THE THREADS THAT GOVERN THE LIVES OF ALL BEINGS, BE THEY MORTAL OR DIVINE.
GATHER ROUND AND LISTEN AS WE SPIN THE TALE OF ATHENA, GREAT GODDESS OF WISDOM AND WAR, DAUGHTER OF ZEUS, THE KING OF THE GODS.

WITH KRONOS THE TITAN, THE ALL-DEVOURING, THE RULER OF ALL THAT WAS.

CURSED BY GAEA, MOTHER EARTH, TO SURRENDER HIS REIGN TO ONE OF HIS CHILDREN, KRONOS INSTEAD SWALLOWED THEM, ONE BY ONE AS THEY WERE BORN.

ALL EXCEPT HIS YOUNGEST, ZEUS, WHO, HIDDEN IN A CAVE ON THE ISLE OF CRETE, SECRETLY GREW TO ADULTHOOD.

HER STORY BEGINS MANY, MANY YEARS AGO, BEFORE HER MOST UNUSUAL BIRTH...

IT WAS THERE THAT ZEUS MET METIS, DAUGHTER OF THE OCEAN, AND THE EVENTUAL MOTHER OF PALLAS ATHENA.
METIS WAS THE ONE WHO GAVE ZEUS THE PLAN TO FREE HIS BROTHERS AND SISTERS FROM KRONOS'S BELLY.

LATER HE LED THEM IN A FINAL BATTLE AGAINST THE TITANS,

A BATTLE THAT ENDED WITH ZEUS AND HIS SIBLINGS AS THE NEW LORDS OF CREATION, AND KRONOS AND HIS FELLOW TITANS IMPRISONED DEEP WITHIN THE BOWELS OF THE EARTH.

BUT MOTHER EARTH LOVED ALL OF HER CHILDREN...
AND SO SHE PROPHESIED AGAINST ZEUS, AS SHE HAD AGAINST KRONOS—

AS YOU HAVE OVERTHROWN YOUR FATHER, SO SHALL YOUR CHILD BY METIS OVERTHROW YOU!

FAR AWAY, IN GREECE, TOWERED MOUNT OLYMPUS, THE TALLEST MOUNTAIN LEFT STANDING AFTER THE CLASH OF GODS AND TITANS.
AND THERE IT WAS THAT ZEUS, THE NEWLY CROWNED KING OF THE GODS, MADE HIS HOME WITH METIS, HIS QUEEN, AND HIS BROTHERS AND SISTERS, THE OLYMPIANS.

ZEUS KNEW ALL TOO WELL THE DOOM THAT A PROPHECY FROM MOTHER EARTH COULD BRING.

AND SO IT WAS THAT ZEUS, THE LORD OF ALL THAT WAS, WAS TROUBLED.

MY HUSBAND, WHAT FURROWS YOUR BROW?
IS THERE ANY COUNSEL I MIGHT OFFER?
BUT ZEUS COULD NOT SHARE THE REASON FOR HIS SILENCE WITH METIS.
AND, BESIDES, HE HAD...
OTHER DISTRACTIONS...

ZEUS DEVELOPED A CUNNING PLAN, A PLAN TO FOOL HIS WIFE, THE GODDESS OF GOOD COUNSEL...

WHAT'S GOTTEN INTO YOU, ZEUS?
I WANT TO GET SOME FRESH AIR! HURRY!

FOLLOW ME!
C'MON!

BUT...
YOU KNOW I CAN'T TRANSFORM AS EASILY AS YOU...

IT'S JUST LIKE I SHOWED YOU, METIS! TRY!
O-OKAY...

YOU CAN DO IT!

CONCENTRATE...

I DID IT!!
ZEUS, I DID IT!!

I KNEW YOU COULD!
NOW LET'S HAVE SOME FUN!

I'LL CHANGE SHAPE, AND YOU FOLLOW ME. READY?
I-I GUESS SO!

HERE WE GO!
RAVEN!
I DID IT AGAIN! IT'S SO MUCH EASI-
BAT!
SOMETHING TRICKIER! SERPENT!
HAHA!
NOW: EAGLE!
WHOOP!
TRY SOMETHING HARDER!
DRAGONFLY!
I DID IT!
I DID IT, ZEUS!

ZEUS?

BUT THAT WAS NOT THE END OF METIS...

HELLO? W-WHERE AM I?
METIS? IT'S ME.
ZEUS.
ZEUS? ZEUS, WHAT HAVE YOU DONE?

I DID WHAT I HAD TO DO, METIS. GAEA SAID OUR CHILD WOULD OVERTHROW ME. I COULDN'T LET THAT HAPPEN.
BUT- BUT WE CAN WORK—
AND I COULDN'T LET YOU GO, METIS. I NEED YOU. I NEVER COULD HAVE OVERTHROWN KRONOS WITHOUT YOU.
ZEUS, WHAT DID Y-

NOW YOU'RE INSIDE ME, A PART OF ME. NOW WE'LL ALWAYS BE TOGETHER.
YOU—YOU CAN'T DO THIS TO ME! ZEUS!

YOU CAN'T DO THIS TO MEEEEEE!!!!!!

BUT ZEUS DID NOT LET HER OUT, AND DESPITE WANTING TO ALWAYS KEEP HER NEAR, ZEUS SOON FORGOT TO LISTEN TO THAT VOICE IN HIS HEAD.

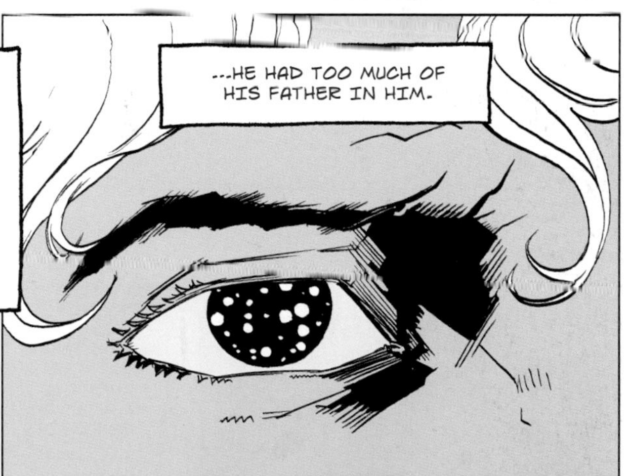
...HE HAD TOO MUCH OF HIS FATHER IN HIM.

FOR ZEUS, THE WORLD CONTINUED WITHOUT METIS.
HE TOOK HERA AS HIS NEW QUEEN, AND THE ENTIRE WORLD CELEBRATED THEIR UNION.
MEANWHILE, UNKNOWN TO EVERYONE, DEEP IN ZEUS'S HEAD, METIS WAS PREGNANT WITH HIS CHILD.

HERA AND ZEUS HAD CHILDREN OF THEIR OWN. THE NUMBER OF GODS ON OLYMPUS BEGAN TO GROW.

AND IN THE SUBCONSCIOUS OF ZEUS, METIS GAVE BIRTH TO HER OWN CHILD, A DAUGHTER.
THIS CHILD INHERITED ALL HER MOTHER'S WISDOM AND INTELLIGENCE, AND HER FATHER'S POWER AND FEROCITY.

IN THE WORLD BEYOND OLYMPUS, THE POPULATION OF MORTAL MEN SWELLED. THEY SPREAD OUT TO ALL THE CORNERS OF THE EARTH, AND BUILT GREAT SHIPS, ARMIES, AND CITIES.

WHILE IN THE HEAD OF ZEUS, METIS'S DAUGHTER SPENT HER DAYS LEARNING THE ARTS AND SCIENCES, AND HER NIGHTS FIGHTING THE WORRIES AND ANXIETIES IN THE DREAMS OF THE KING OF GODS.

AND IN HUMAN CITIES, MEN BUILT TEMPLES AND MONUMENTS AND MADE SACRIFICES TO THE GODS OF OLYMPUS, WHO SERVED AS THEIR PROTECTORS AND THEIR INSPIRATION.

CLANG
CLANG
SENSING THE TIME WAS NEAR, METIS WORKED DAY AND NIGHT, POURING THE LAST OF HER ESSENCE INTO THE APPROPRIATE CLOTHING FOR HER DAUGHTER'S DEBUT ON OLYMPUS.

UNTIL, FINALLY:
CLANG
CLANG
CLANG
CLANG
AAAAAH MY POUNDING SKULL!!!!

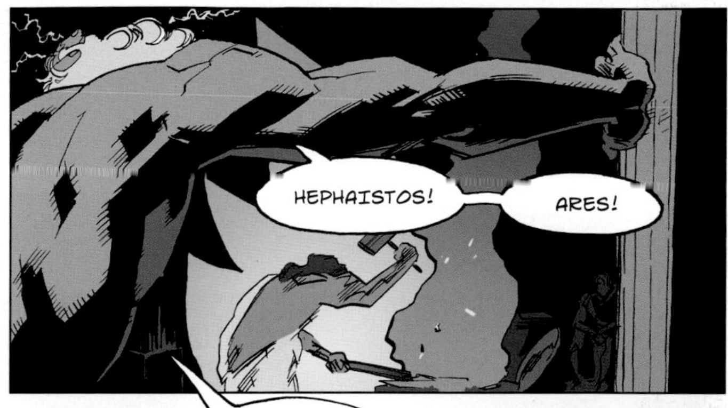
HEPHAISTOS!
ARES!

I NEED YOUR HELP!

A QUICK DIAGNOSIS; A PLAN WAS HATCHED.
TO EASE THE INCESSANT POUNDING AND PRESSURE, HEPHAISTOS WOULD CLEAVE THE SKULL OF ZEUS WITH A HAMMER AND SPIKE.
THE BLOW WAS STRUCK.
KLANK!

AND SO IT WAS THAT THE WORLD MET ATHENA AS SHE SPRANG FORTH FROM HER FATHER'S SPLIT SKULL, FULLY CLOTHED, FULLY ARMED, ALREADY A YOUNG WOMAN.
SHE SCREAMED, AND HER GREY EYES FLASHED THE COLOR OF ZEUS'S STORM CLOUDS.
HER YELL WAS NOT THE CRY OF A NEWBORN BABE,
BUT RATHER THE SHOUT OF A WARRIOR.

ZEUS, BEING ZEUS, HEALED INSTANTLY. HIS HEAD ACHED NO MORE THAN ANY FATHER'S HEAD DOES FOR HIS CHILD. BUT HER MIRACULOUS BIRTH, HER PRE-LIFE GESTATION IN HER FATHER'S SKULL, CHANGED ATHENA.
SHE HAD BEEN PROPHESIED TO END HER FATHER'S RULE, BUT ATHENA INSTEAD BECAME HIS STAUNCHEST ALLY, HIS FAVORITE CHILD.
ZEUS HAD MANAGED TO TURN BACK THE FATES. BUT MOTHER EARTH WOULD NOT REST EASILY...
AN EXCELLENT STORY TO BE SURE, SISTER KLOTHOS.
INDEED.
NOW I WILL PICK UP THE THREAD OF THE TALE, AND EXPLAIN HOW ATHENA CAME TO USE THE NAME PALLAS.

NEWLY BORN, BUT A YOUNG WOMAN, ATHENA FOUND IT DIFFICULT TO FIT IN AT OLYMPUS.
THOUGH A WARRIOR, SHE HAD LITTLE IN COMMON WITH HER HALF-BROTHER ARES, THE BLOODTHIRSTY GOD OF WAR.
A WEAVER OF UNSURPASSED SKILL, SHE COULD NOT ENDURE THE HEAT, CLAMOR, AND SOOT OF HEPHAISTOS'S WORKSHOP.
AND IN CHILDREN, AND THE MAKING OF CHILDREN, SHE HAD NO INTEREST.

SO ATHENA SET OUT TO FIND HER PLACE IN THE WORLD.

IN THE COUNTRY OF LIBYA, TRITON, THE SON OF POSEIDON, OPERATED A CAMP FOR THE TRAINING OF WARRIORS.

THERE ATHENA TRAINED AND SPARRED, COMPETED, AND BATTLED WITH YOUNG WOMEN OF DIVINE AND SEMI-DIVINE BIRTH.

WITHOUT A MOTHER AND DENIED ANY SEMBLANCE OF A NORMAL CHILDHOOD, ATHENA HOPED TO DISCOVER SOMETHING ABOUT WHO SHE WAS, AND HER PLACE IN THE WORLD AMONG THE YOUNG WARRIORS AT TRITON'S CAMP.
WHAT BETTER PLACE FOR THE GODDESS OF WAR TO FIND HERSELF?

WHAT DOES SHE SAY?
SHE SAYS MY FATHER HAS ARRIVED.
WE'D BETTER HEAD BACK TO CAMP.

WHAT'S HE LIKE?
WHO?
ZEUS, OF COURSE! YOUR FATHER!
OH, YOU KNOW, LIKE ANY DAD.

WHAT ABOUT YOUR MOTHER? WHAT'S HERA LIKE?
OH NO, HERA'S NOT MY MOTHER.
I SUPPOSE ZEUS HAS HAD MANY LOVERS!—
I DON'T HAVE A MOTHER. MY FATHER GAVE BIRTH TO ME, ALONE, FROM HIS HEAD.

WHAT? HOW COULD HE? MEN DON'T HAVE BABIES! YOU MUST JUST NOT REMEMBER HER.

THAT'S NOT ENTIRELY TRUE. SOMETIMES...
SOMETIMES I CAN ALMOST SEEM TO REMEMBER...

BUT THEN SHE'S GONE. ALL THAT'S LEFT IS A TINY LITTLE VOICE INSIDE MY HEAD, THAT TELLS ME THINGS. GIVES ME ADVICE. SHOWS ME RIGHT FROM WRONG.

OH MY GODS! LOOK! IT'S HIM!

HE'S—HE'S BEAUTIFUL!
ATHENA. DAUGHTER.

HELLO, FATHER.
GREETINGS AND SALUTATIONS, LORD ZEUS!

HELLO, AH—
PALLAS, SIRE. TRITON'S DAUGHTER! POSEIDON'S GRANDDAUGHTER. IT'S AN HONOR TO MEET YOU!

OH! AND LOOK! YOU'RE WEARING THE AEGIS!
WHAT'S THE AEGIS?

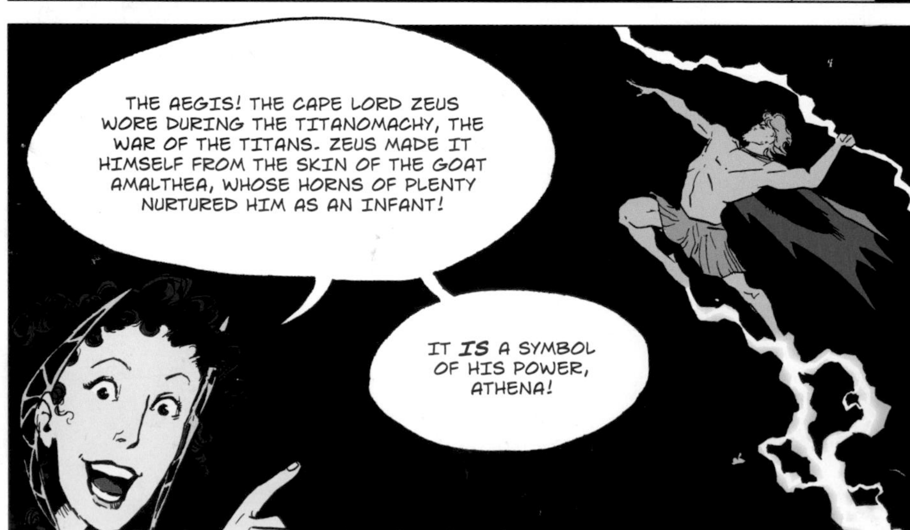
THE AEGIS! THE CAPE LORD ZEUS WORE DURING THE TITANOMACHY, THE WAR OF THE TITANS. ZEUS MADE IT HIMSELF FROM THE SKIN OF THE GOAT AMALTHEA, WHOSE HORNS OF PLENTY NURTURED HIM AS AN INFANT!
IT **IS** A SYMBOL OF HIS POWER, ATHENA!

MY FATHER IS HOLDING GAMES IN YOUR HONOR TOMORROW, LORD ZEUS!
I WILL FIGHT IN YOUR HONOR AS YOUR CHAMPION!

...VERY EAGER, THAT PALLAS.
SHE'S TOO YOUNG FOR YOU, FATHER.

PARDON?
NOTHING.

HOW ARE YOU, MY DAUGHTER?
I AM WELL, FATHER.
AND ARE YOU HAPPY HERE?
YES, VERY HAPPY.

THAT'S GOOD... DO YOU THINK...
DO YOU THINK THAT YOU MIGHT RETURN TO OLYMPUS?

YOU ARE MY FAVORITE CHILD. YOU SHOULD BE WITH ME THERE, AT MY SIDE.
MY CLOSEST ALLY. MY TRUEST CHILD.

NOT YET, MY FATHER.
THERE IS STILL MUCH THAT I MUST LEARN HERE.

I UNDERSTAND.
KNOW THIS, MY DAUGHTER, THERE IS ALWAYS A THRONE FOR YOU ON OLYMPUS.

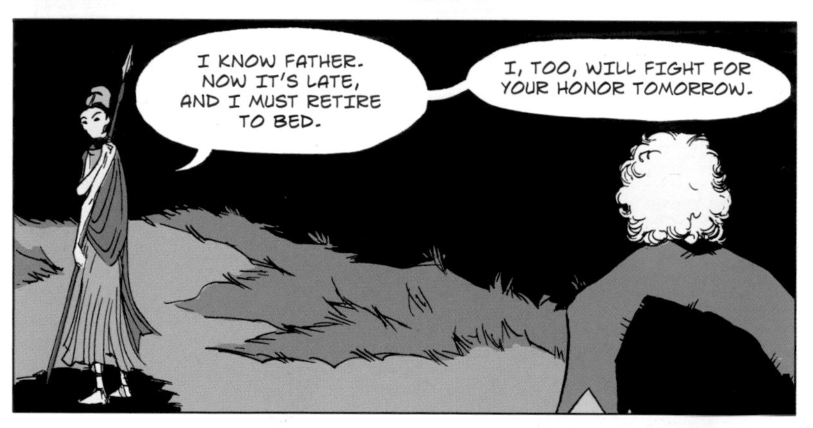
I KNOW FATHER. NOW IT'S LATE, AND I MUST RETIRE TO BED.
I, TOO, WILL FIGHT FOR YOUR HONOR TOMORROW.

IN THE MORNING THE GAMES BEGAN.
ATHENA HAD SPENT THE NIGHT WITH THE OTHER GIRLS IN THE BARRACKS. SHE ROSE AND COMPETED WITH THEM.

THERE WERE CONTESTS OF ARCHERY

OF DISCUS THROWING

OF RUNNING

OF SWORDPLAY.

THE DAY WORE ON AND EVENTUALLY THERE WERE ONLY TWO CONTESTANTS LEFT:
ATHENA
AND PALLAS.
BOTH FOUGHT FOR ZEUS, THOUGH FOR DIFFERENT REASONS. THE GAMES WOULD BE OVER, THE VICTOR DECIDED, WHEN ONE OF THEM HAD DISARMED THE OTHER.

TRITON SIGNALED FOR THE MATCH TO BEGIN.
IT MIGHT BE ASSUMED THAT, AS A YOUNG GODDESS OF WAR AND DAUGHTER OF ZEUS, ATHENA WOULD FIND THIS AN EASY VICTORY.

BUT THIS CONTEST WAS FOUGHT WITH THE SPEAR, THE VERY WEAPON PALLAS HAD TRAINED WITH SINCE SHE COULD WALK.
HER GRANDFATHER, POSEIDON, HAD FOUGHT IN THE TITANOMACHY WITH THE THREE-HEADED SPEAR CALLED THE TRIDENT. HER FATHER TRITON HAD A TRIDENT AS WELL. IT WAS IN HER BLOOD.

IN THIS CONTEST AT LEAST, THEY WERE EVENLY MATCHED.
THE BATTLE WENT ON AND ON, BACK AND FORTH.
FIRST ATHENA SEEMED TO HAVE THE UPPER HAND,
THEN PALLAS.
ZEUS GREW CONCERNED.
THOUGH FLATTERED BY PALLAS'S ATTENTIONS, HE DID NOT WANT TO SEE HIS DAUGHTER LOSE.

HE RECALLED PALLAS'S ATTRACTION TO HIS AEGIS.
HE FLICKED IT OUT, HOPING TO DISTRACT PALLAS, TO GIVE ATHENA A CHANCE TO DISARM HER.

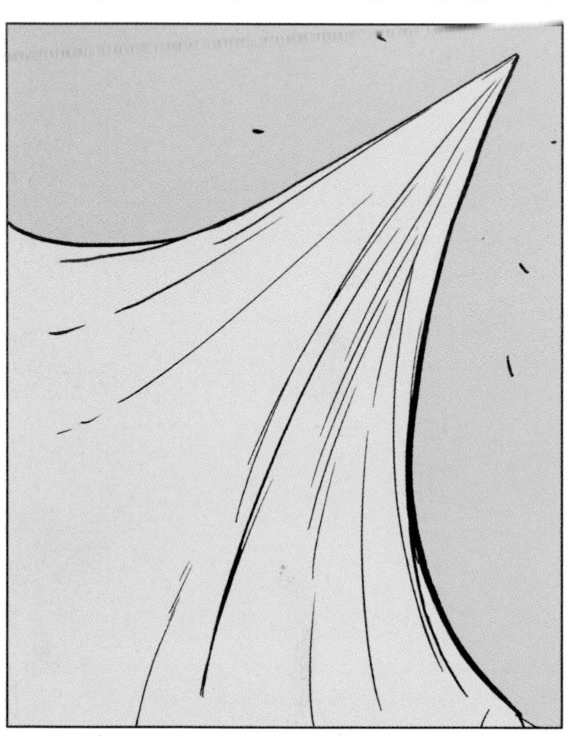

IT WORKED. TOO WELL.

PALLAS! OH PALLAS! HOW DID THIS HAPPEN?!
ATHENA?
OH PALLAS, I'M SO SORRY!—
D-DID ZEUS SEE HOW I FOUGHT FOR HIM...

THAT NIGHT, INSTEAD OF A FEAST, THERE WAS A FUNERAL FOR PALLAS.
NO ONE, NOT EVEN TRITON, BLAMED ATHENA. IT WAS AN ACCIDENT.
A CRUEL TWIST OF FATE.

THAT WAS NO CONSOLATION FOR ATHENA. SHE KNEW THE ANGER SHE HAD FELT.

THE ANGER OVER PALLAS'S INFATUATION WITH HER FATHER.

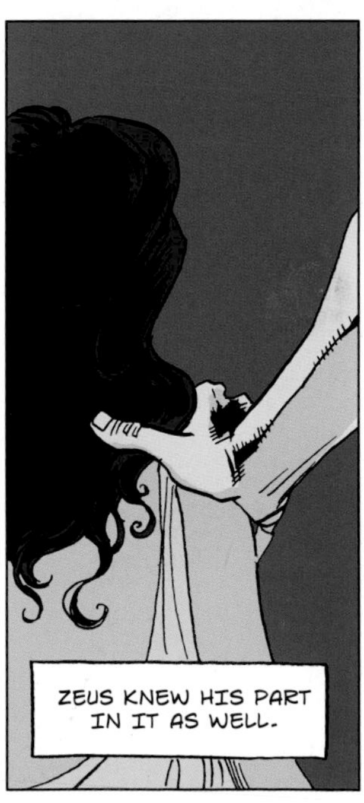
ZEUS KNEW HIS PART IN IT AS WELL.

HE MADE AMENDS
THE ONLY WAY HE
COULD THINK OF.

AND THAT IS HOW ATHENA CAME TO BE GIFTED WITH HER MOST POTENT WEAPON, THE AEGIS.
TO HONOR HER FALLEN FRIEND AND TO NEVER FORGET THE ANGER THAT LED TO PALLAS'S DEATH, ATHENA TOOK ON HER NAME.
SHE LEARNED TO NEVER AGAIN LET ANGER CLOUD HER JUDGMENT IN BATTLE. SHE WOULD ALWAYS USE HER GOOD COUNSEL.

ANOTHER TALE WELL TOLD, SISTER LAKHESIS.
I HAVE ANOTHER THREAD TO ADD TO OUR TAPESTRY.

ANOTHER TALE, ANOTHER PALLAS.
AND, CURIOUSLY, ANOTHER TALE OF THE AEGIS.

IT IS FITTING, MY SISTERS, THAT WE TELL THIS TALE HERE IN THE GRAVEYARD OF GIANTS.
THESE STONES, THESE BROKEN, JAGGED FORMS, ARE ALL THAT REMAIN TO MARK THE END OF ANOTHER OF MOTHER EARTH'S ATTEMPTS TO END THE OLYMPIAN ORDER.
BY THIS TIME, ATHENA HAD CLAIMED HER PROMISED THRONE ON OLYMPUS...

BOOM
BOOM
BOOM

THOOM! THOOM! THOOM!
BOOM
BOOM
BOO

HOLD.
DO YOU NOT HEAR?
BOOM
BOOM

BOOM

BOOM

THE GIGANTOMACHY.
THE BATTLE OF THE GIGANTES.
BROTHERS OF A SORT TO US, BORN OF THE MINGLING OF MOTHER EARTH AND THE SPILLED BLOOD OF OURANOS, THE SKY.
NEVER HAVING FORGIVEN ZEUS FOR IMPRISONING THE TITANS, GAEA FED THE EARTH-BORN GIGANTES, AND THEY SWELLED TO ENORMOUS SIZES.
WITH WHISPERED LIES AND TRUTHS SHE LIKEWISE TURNED THEIR RAGE AND JEALOUSY OF THE OLYMPIANS INTO A WHITE-HOT INFERNO.
LIKE A CRUDE MOCKERY OF THE TITANS, THE GIGANTES FOCUSED THEIR FURY ON MOUNT OLYMPUS. THE GIGANTES RIPPED UP MOUNTAIN AFTER MOUNTAIN, AND STACKED EACH ATOP ONE ANOTHER TO MATCH THE PEERLESS HEIGHT OF MIGHTY OLYMPUS.

GAEA HAS TOLD US, OLYMPIANS,

HOW YOU LOOK DOWN ON US, FROM YOUR THRONES ON HIGH
BOOM

THINK YOU'RE BETTER THAN US!
YEAH!

OLYMPUS WILL FALL TO US!

I KNOW GRANDMOTHER EARTH CRAVES MY DEFEAT—
KRAKA BOOM!

BUT SHE'LL HAVE TO DO BETTER THAN YOU!

FOLLOW MY LEAD!
WE'LL DRIVE THEM BACK FROM OLYMPUS!

PUSH THEM BACK
PUSH THEM
BACK!!!
AARH!
NO!
HURK!

tHRUNK
WHUD
SLAM!

IS THAT IT? HAVE THEY BEEN DEFEATED?

GRARGGHH!
RRRRAARGH!
LOOK! THE FALLEN GIANTS DRAW NEW STRENGTH FROM MOTHER EARTH!

STRIKE THEM DOWN! CUT THEM TO PIECES!

THEY RETURN TO THE ROCKS AND STONES THAT SPAWNED THEM!

HAH!

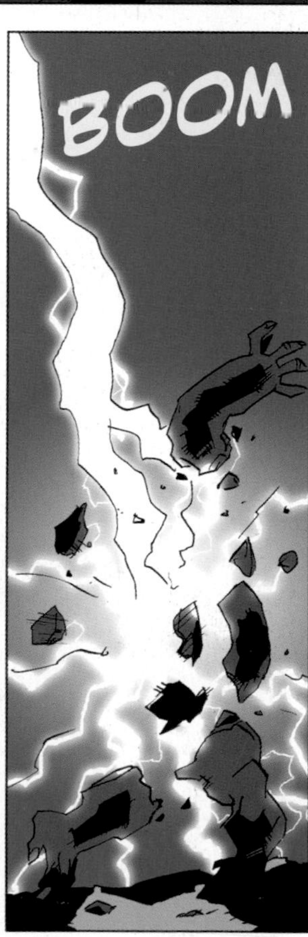
BOOM

"STRIKE THEM DOWN"? THAT'S HOW SHE LEADS?

WHAT DOES SHE THINK I'VE BEEN DO—
—ING.

KRAK!

WHICH OLYMPIAN WILL FALL BEFORE ME NEXT?
WHICH OLYMPIAN WILL FALL BEFORE... PALLAS?
PALLAS, HUH?
YOU'RE MINE.

AA-THEE-NA.

YOU'RE VERY BRAVE TO FACE ME, GIRL.

OR VERY STUPID.

MOTHER EARTH HERSELF HAS MADE IT SO THAT...

...NO BLADE CAN PIERCE MY SKIN AS LONG AS I LIVE.

LOOKS LIKE I'LL HAVE TO GET CREATIVE, THEN.

GRAARRRR!
HUP!
THIS PALLAS WAS THE LEADER OF THE GIGANTES (IF SUCH AS THE GIGANTES COULD BE SAID TO HAVE A LEADER).

MOTHER EARTH HAD GROWN HIS STRENGTH AND STATURE TO TRULY TITANIC PROPORTIONS.

HUH? WHAT?

GET OFF!!

YOU KNOW, PALLAS...

I THINK YOUR SCALY HIDE WOULD BE A NICE ADDITION TO MY AEGIS.
NO!

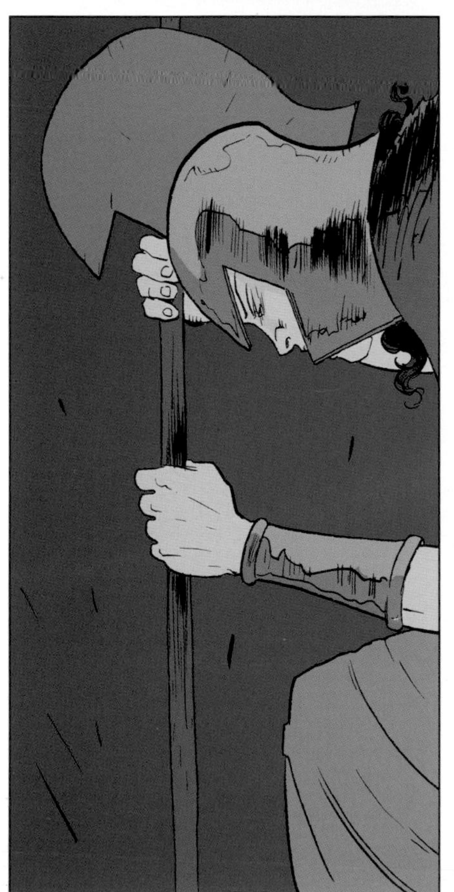

GNFF!

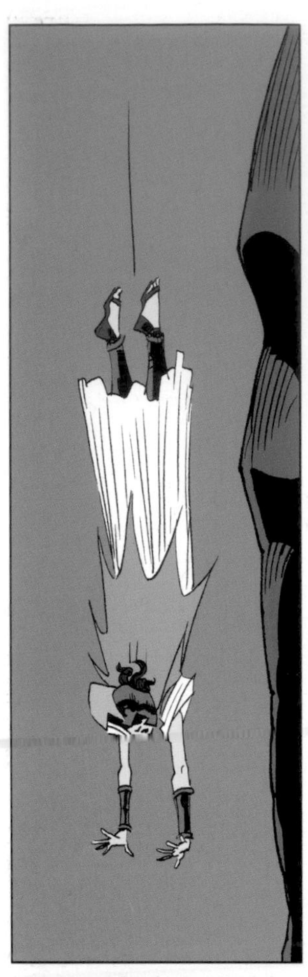

OOF!

"NO BLADE CAN PIERCE MY SKIN AS LONG AS I LIVE," HUH?

NICE.... VERY NICE....
STILL NEEDS A LITTLE SOMETHING, THOUGH...

LEADERLESS, THE REST OF THE BATTLE WENT POORLY FOR THE GIGANTES
THE OLYMPIANS ROUTED THEM, AND THE LANDSCAPE WAS COVERED WITH THEIR ENORMOUS CORPSES:
NEW MOUNTAINS TO REPLACE THE ONES THE GIGANTES TORE UP.

GAEA LEARNED FROM THIS DEFEAT. WHEN NEXT SHE ROSE UP AGAINST ZEUS, SHE WOULD BE READY.

TRUE TO HER WORD, ATHENA ADDED THE PELT OF PALLAS TO HER AEGIS.
IT PROVED QUITE AS IMPENETRABLE FOR HER AFTER PALLAS'S DEATH AS IT HAD FOR HIM IN LIFE.

THERE ARE SOME WHO SAY THAT THIS GRISLY ADDITION TO THE AEGIS IS WHY SHE IS KNOWN AS PALLAS ATHENA,
AND WHO IS TO SAY THAT THEY ARE WRONG?
HERE IS ANOTHER TALE OF ATHENA AND HER AEGIS. ANOTHER TALE OF FATE, AND THE RUIN THAT IS VISITED UPON THOSE WHO EVADE THEIR OWN.

IT IS A STORY OF THE WRATH OF GODS, AND ALSO OF THEIR FAVOR.
WE TELL IT TO YOU NOW.

IN A DISTANT ISLAND TEMPLE, DEDICATED TO ATHENA, THERE LIVED A BEAUTIFUL YOUNG PRIESTESS NAMED MEDUSA.
LIKE ALL OF ATHENA'S PRIESTESSES, SHE DEVOTED HERSELF ENTIRELY TO THE GODDESS. SHE WOULD NEVER MARRY AND NEVER HAVE CHILDREN.

UNFORTUNATELY FOR MEDUSA, HER BEAUTY CAUGHT THE EYE OF POSEIDON, GOD OF THE SEA.

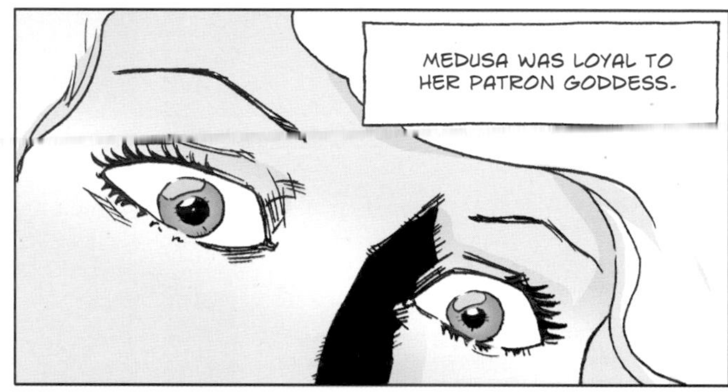
MEDUSA WAS LOYAL TO HER PATRON GODDESS.

BUT WHAT WOMAN CAN LONG RESIST A GOD'S EMBRACE?

SHE TOOK POSEIDON AS HER LOVER, AND ATHENA'S TEMPLE BECAME THEIR SECRET HIDEAWAY.
TO SAY THIS DISPLEASED ATHENA WOULD BE AN UNDERSTATEMENT.

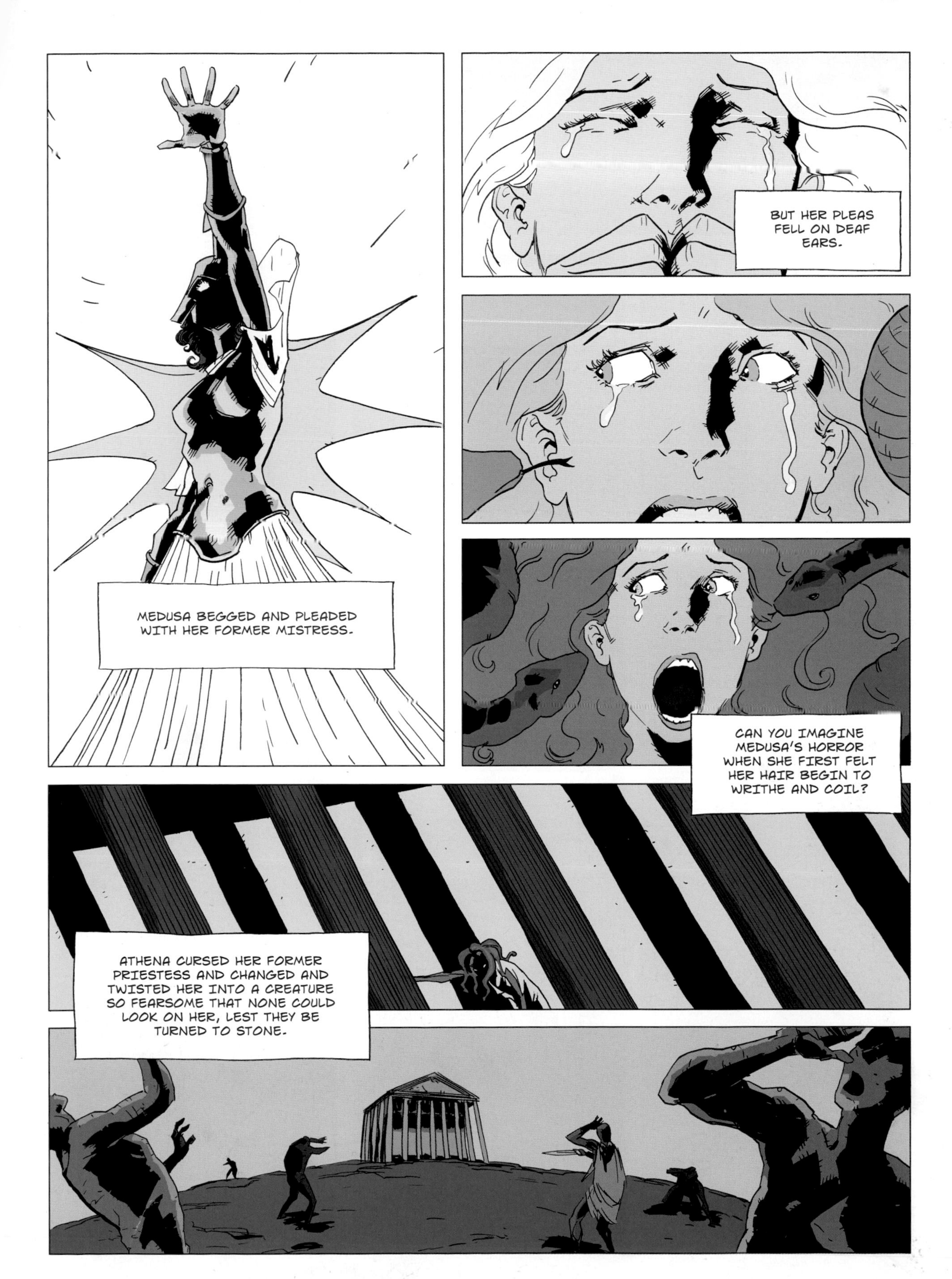
MEDUSA BEGGED AND PLEADED WITH HER FORMER MISTRESS.
BUT HER PLEAS FELL ON DEAF EARS.
CAN YOU IMAGINE MEDUSA'S HORROR WHEN SHE FIRST FELT HER HAIR BEGIN TO WRITHE AND COIL?
ATHENA CURSED HER FORMER PRIESTESS AND CHANGED AND TWISTED HER INTO A CREATURE SO FEARSOME THAT NONE COULD LOOK ON HER, LEST THEY BE TURNED TO STONE.

POSEIDON, FOR HIS PART, SLUNK BACK TO THE SEA.
WHEN GODS TANGLE WITH MORTALS, IT IS SELDOM THE GODS WHO PAY.

ANOTHER THREAD OF THIS TALE: THE MORTAL PRINCESS DANAE, DAUGHTER OF ACRISIUS, KING OF ARGOS.
FATED TO BEAR A SON WHO WOULD OVERTHROW HER FATHER

ACRISIUS LOCKED HER HIGH IN A TOWER TO SAFEGUARD HIS RULE.
BUT THIS ONLY BROUGHT HER CLOSER TO THE GODS.

CALLING UP HIS CLOUDS, ZEUS TOOK THE FORM OF A GOLDEN RAIN, AND SEEPED INTO DANAE'S TOWER ROOM.

ZEUS WAS WITH HER THERE, AND SHE BECAME PREGNANT.

MONTHS LATER, ALERTED BY THE CRIES OF AN INFANT, ACRISIUS DISCOVERED HIS DAUGHTER HAD PRODUCED A SON.

RIGHTLY SUSPECTING DIVINE INVOLVEMENT, ACRISIUS DIDN'T KILL THE BOY.
RATHER HE SEALED MOTHER AND SON IN A CASKET OF BRONZE AND SET THEM TO SEA.

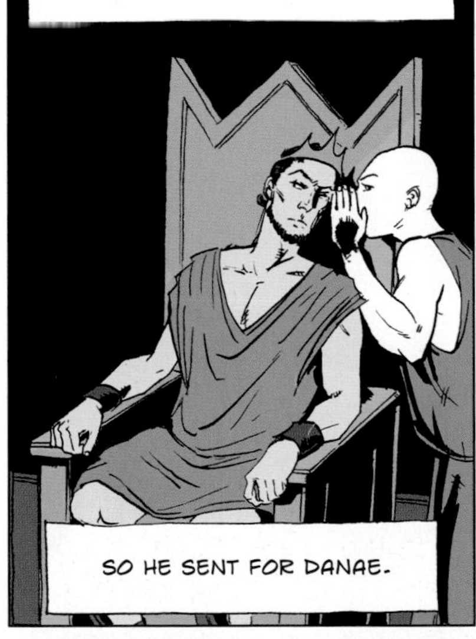

POLYDEKTES WANTED TO MAKE DANAE HIS BRIDE, BUT HE WANTED NO FALSE HEIR TO HIS THRONE...

HE HAD TO GET RID OF PERSEUS SOMEHOW.

POLYDEKTES DEMANDED A WEDDING GIFT FROM HIS STEPSON-TO-BE:

THE HEAD OF MEDUSA THE GORGON.

AND SO IT WAS THAT PERSEUS, MORTAL SON OF ZEUS, FOUND HIMSELF IN THE LARGEST CITY OF SERIPHOS, LOOKING FOR SOMEONE TO GUIDE HIM TO MEDUSA.

BREAD! JUST BAKED THIS MORNING!
OLIVES! GET YOUR OLIVES HERE!
FIGS! FINEST IN THE LAND!

BOY! HEY, BOY! YOU LOOK LIKE YOU HAVE SOMEWHERE IMPORTANT TO BE!
...I DO...BUT I DON'T KNOW WHERE IT IS...
A QUEST, THEN! YOU HAVE THE LOOK OF SOMEONE ON A VERY IMPORTANT QUEST.

OFF TO SLAY SOME MONSTER, I WAGER. A KINGLY QUEST, THAT WOULD BE, HMMM?
HOW DID YOU KNOW?
I'M OLDER THAN I LOOK! I KNOW A LOT OF THINGS! COME INSIDE MY SHOP! I HAVE JUST WHAT YOU NEED!

COME AROUND BACK! COME, COME!

THIS WAY, THIS WAY.

HELLO?

NOT VERY WISE.
ENTERING A DARKENED DOORWAY WITHOUT KNOWING WHAT LIES BEHIND.

GODS.
LADY ATHENA, LORD HERMES, I AM YOUR HUMB—
RISE, PERSEUS. YOU ARE BLOOD TO US.

WE THREE SHARE THE SAME FATHER. AT HIS REQUEST, HERMES AND I ARE TO HELP YOU ON YOUR APPOINTED JOURNEY.

POLYDEKTES HAS SENT YOU ON A FOOL'S ERRAND. EVEN IN DEATH, THE GAZE OF MEDUSA IS LETHAL.
WITHOUT OUR HELP, YOU WILL SURELY FAIL. ALL I ASK IN RETURN IS THAT YOU BRING THE HEAD OF MEDUSA THE GORGON TO ME.
HERMES?
LET'S SEE...

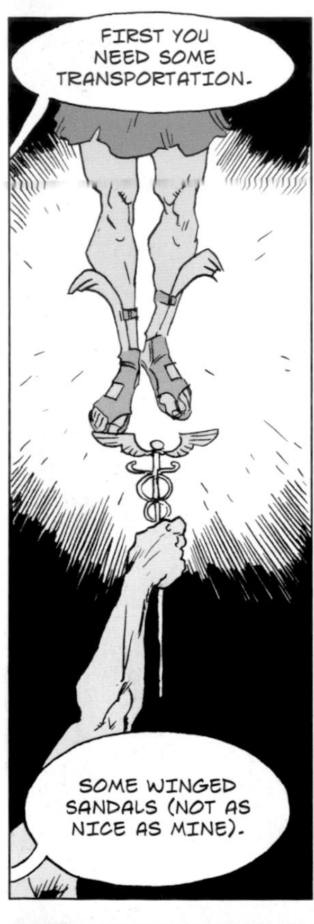
FIRST YOU NEED SOME TRANSPORTATION.
SOME WINGED SANDALS (NOT AS NICE AS MINE).

IT IS VITAL YOU MUST NEVER LOOK MEDUSA IN THE FACE. MAKE SURE THAT YOU ONLY GLIMPSE HER IN THIS POLISHED SHIELD.

THIS IS THE SWORD I USED TO CUT OFF THE HEAD OF ARGUS PANOPTES, THE ALL-SEEING.
(HE DIDN'T SEE THAT COMING). IT SHOULD SERVE YOU WELL HERE.

ANYTHING ELSE WE CAN GET YOU?
UH... A HELMET OF INVISIBILITY?
AHAHAHAHA—NO.

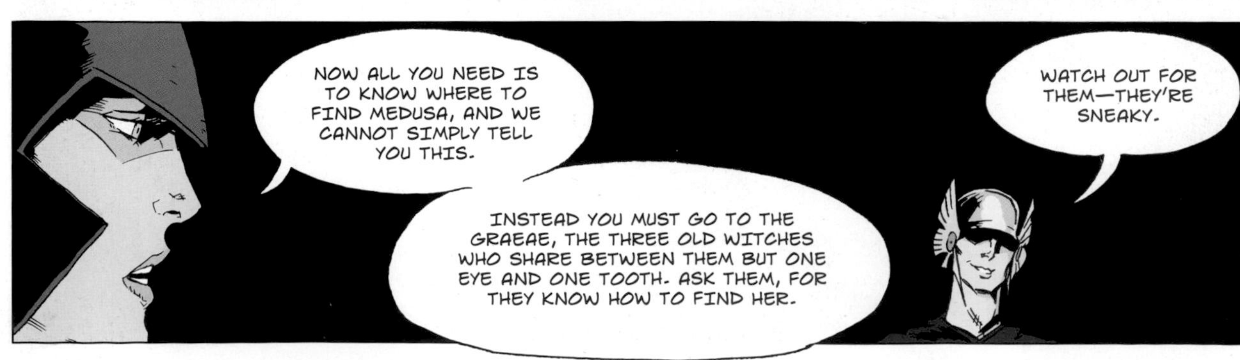
NOW ALL YOU NEED IS TO KNOW WHERE TO FIND MEDUSA, AND WE CANNOT SIMPLY TELL YOU THIS.
INSTEAD YOU MUST GO TO THE GRAEAE, THE THREE OLD WITCHES WHO SHARE BETWEEN THEM BUT ONE EYE AND ONE TOOTH. ASK THEM, FOR THEY KNOW HOW TO FIND HER.
WATCH OUT FOR THEM—THEY'RE SNEAKY.

WHY COULD ATHENA NOT JUST TELL PERSEUS HOW TO FIND MEDUSA? SURELY SHE KNEW THE WAY.

'TIS BEST NOT TO QUESTION THE MOTIVES OF THE GODS.
WHUFF!

IT LOOKS)

YOU'RE STIRRING TOO QUICKLY!
YOU KNOW?
WHO HAS THE EYE?
I DO!

IS THIS TOO THICK, OR TOO THIN?
LET ME SEE...

EEK!

THE EYE! SOMEONE STOLE THE EYE!
ARE YOU SURE? YOU PROBABLY JUST DROPPED IT.
WHAT HAPPENED?
NO! THEY GRABBED IT!

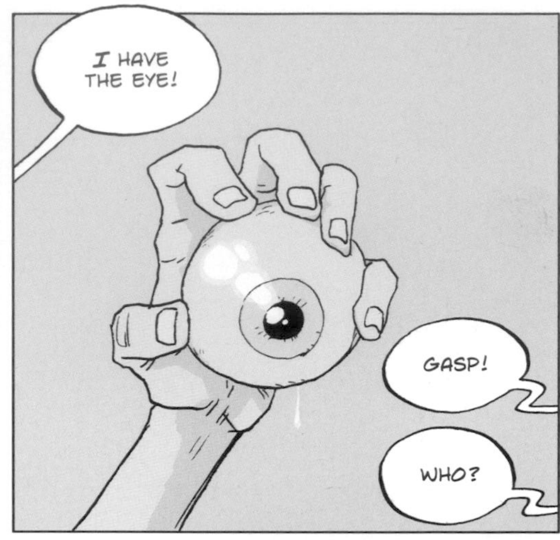
I HAVE THE EYE!
GASP!
WHO?

AND IF YOU EVER WANT TO, UH, SEE IT AGAIN, YOU'LL ANSWER MY QUESTION!
SOMEONE STOLE OUR EYE?!
WHO WOULD DO SUCH A THING?
WHO HAS THE TOOTH?
I DO!
BITE HIM!

GREY LADIES, WILL YOU ANSWER MY QUESTION?
AYE, WE'LL ANSWER YOUR QUESTION AS BEST WE CAN. ONE WONDERS WHAT IT IS THAT HAS YOU SO DESPERATE AS TO STEAL AN OLD WOMAN'S EYE.
I WANNA BITE HIM!
SHHH!

KING POLYDEKTES OF SERIPHOS HAS ORDERED ME TO BRING HIM THE HEAD OF MEDUSA THE GORGON.
I AM PREPARED TO DO THIS, BUT I KNOW NOT WHERE TO BEGIN. HOW, GREY LADIES, DO I FIND THE ISLE OF MEDUSA?

YOU SEEK MEDUSA? IT MIGHT BE BEST IF YOU LEAVE YOUR OWN EYES WITH US, FOR ALL THE GOOD THEY'LL DO YOU. ONE LOOK AT HER FACE AND YOU'LL BE A STATUE!

AND WHAT OF HER SISTERS, THE GORGONS? THEY'LL NOT TURN YOU TO STONE, BUT THEY WILL TEAR YOU LIMB FROM LIMB. YOU'D BEST PRAY TO YOUR GODS THAT YOUR SWORD IS SHARP!

A TREACHEROUS REEF SURROUNDS THE ISLE OF MEDUSA! I HOPE YOU HAVE WINGS ON YOUR ANKLES, FOR I DOUBT YOUR SHIP WILL SURVIVE THE JOURNEY.

IF, DESPITE THESE WARNINGS, GIVEN OUT OF OUR GENUINE CONCERN, YOU STILL WISH TO GO ON YOUR FOOL'S ERRAND, THIS IS THE WAY: JUST FOLLOW THE WINDS OFF THE COAST OF ETHIOPIA. THEY'LL TAKE YOU TO MEDUSA.
WE'VE TOLD YOU WHAT YOU ASKED, THOUGH YOU MAY NOT LIKE THE ANSWERS. NOW... GIVE US OUR EYE BACK.

CATCH!

SUCH A NICE-SOUNDING BOY...
YES...
WE OUGHT TO HAVE HIM FOR DINNER.

FULLY PREPARED AND
NOW FULLY INFORMED,
PERSEUS FLEW TO THE
ISLE OF MEDUSA.

UHF!

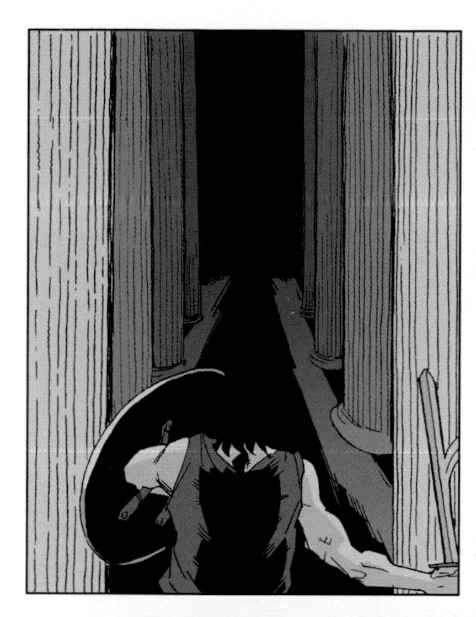

AAH!

HHIIIIIIIIIIIIIIIIIIIISSSSSSSSSSSSS
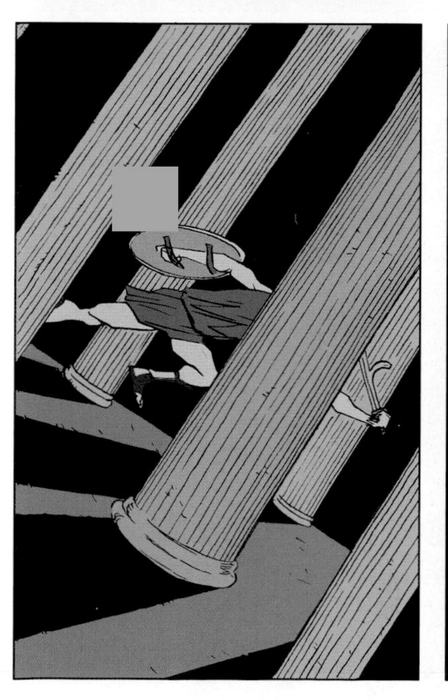

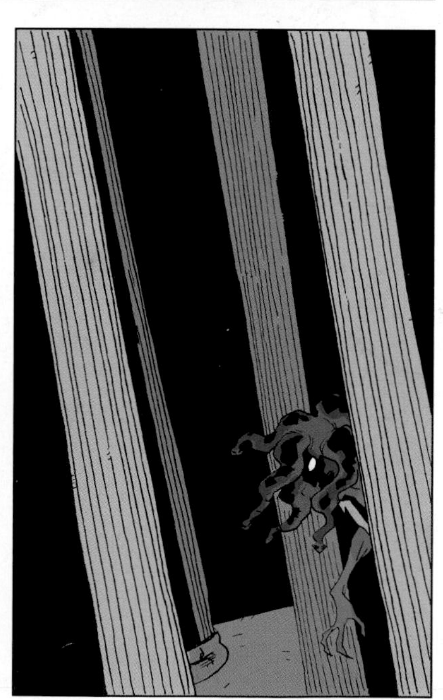

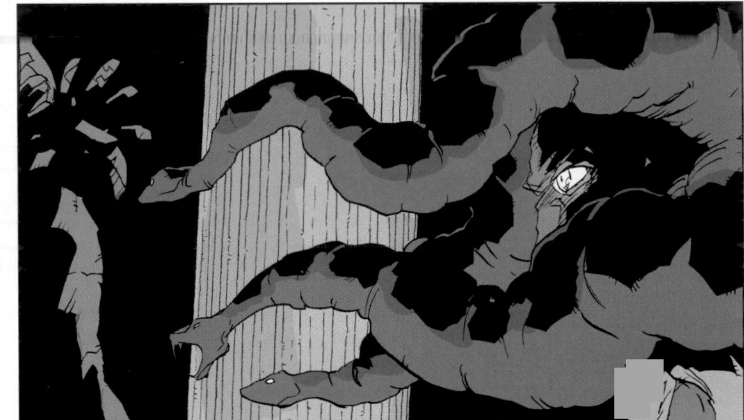

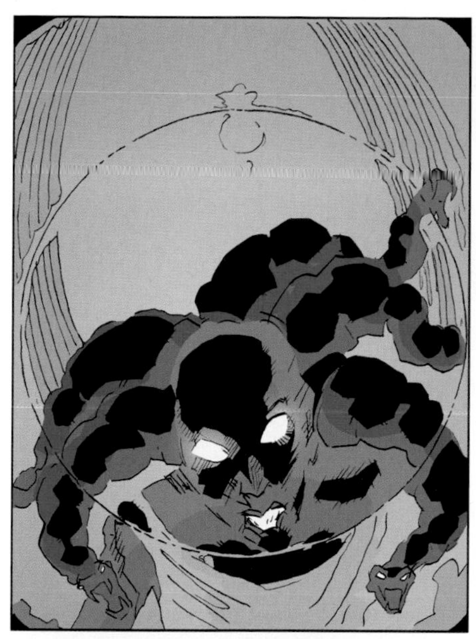

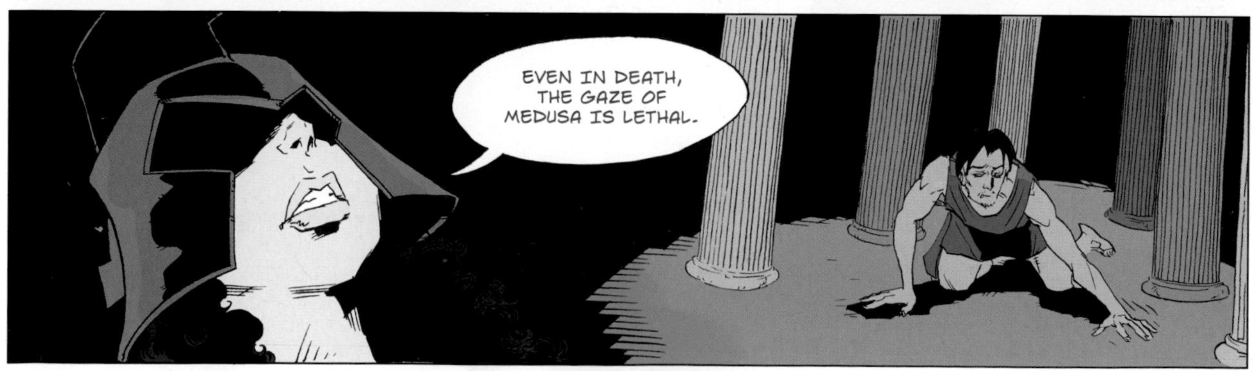
EVEN IN DEATH,
THE GAZE OF
MEDUSA IS LETHAL.

ICK!

AH!

UGH!

DON'T LOOK...

PSHEW!

OH, NO.

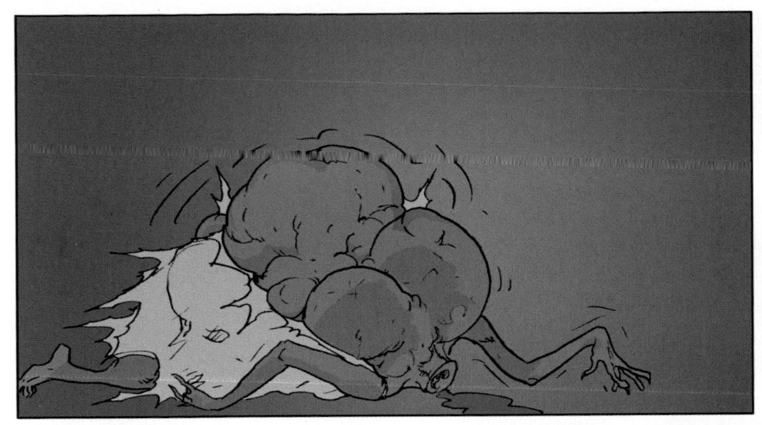
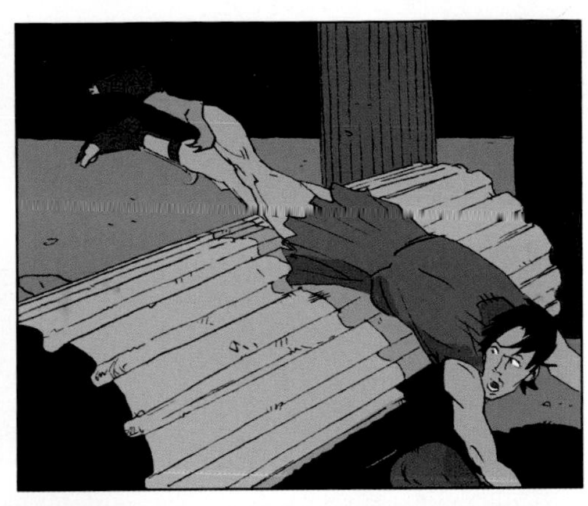

SO BEAUTIFUL...

HISSS!
AAAH!

HIISSS
HIISSS

AS HEROES GO, PERSEUS HAD MORE HELP THAN MOST. IT SEEMS HIS EVERY STEP HAD BEEN GUIDED AND PREORDAINED BY THE GODS.
BUT WHAT HAPPENED NEXT PROVED THE TRUE MEASURE OF HIS HEROISM.

UPON HIS RETURN FROM THE ISLE OF MEDUSA, WHILE APPROACHING ONCE MORE THE COAST OF ETHIOPIA, PERSEUS PERCEIVED AN IMPOSSIBLY ENORMOUS SHAPE BENEATH THE WAVES.
IT WAS THE SEA MONSTER CETUS, SENT BY POSEIDON.
QUEEN KASSIOPEA OF ETHIOPIA BOASTED THAT HER DAUGHTER, ANDROMEDA, WAS MORE BEAUTIFUL THAN THE NYMPHS OF THE SEA.
A SMALL OFFENSE, REALLY.

BUT IT WAS ENOUGH THAT
THE NEREIDS DEMANDED
A SACRIFICE TO RESTORE
THEIR WOUNDED HONOR:

THE DEATH OF
KASSIOPEA'S
DAUGHTER,
ANDROMEDA.

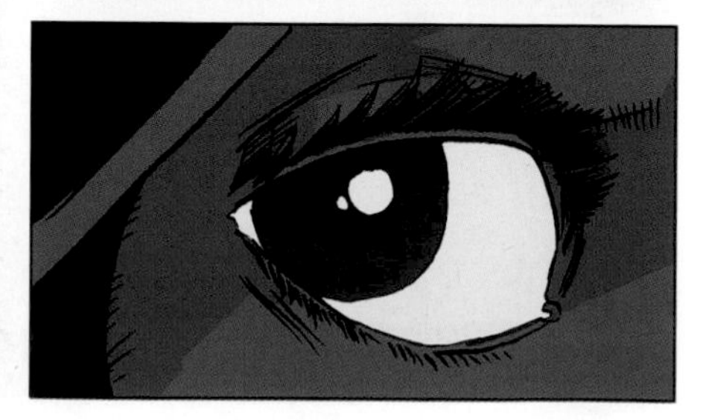

BUT SUCH WAS NOT MEANT TO BE THE FATE OF ANDROMEDA.
HI THERE.
MY NAME'S PERSEUS.

PERSEUS AND THE GRATEFUL ANDROMEDA FELL IN LOVE, AND WERE MARRIED. HE TOOK HER BACK WITH HIM TO SERIPHOS,

WHERE HE USED THE HEAD OF MEDUSA TO PETRIFY POLYDEKTES AND HIS COURT.
HE LEFT THE KINDLY FISHERMAN AS THE NEW KING OF SERIPHOS, AND RETURNED WITH HIS MOTHER AND WIFE TO ARGOS, THE COUNTRY OF HIS BIRTH.

ACRISIUS SAW HIM COMING AND FLED. PERSEUS WAS HAILED AS THE NEW KING OF ARGOS. GAMES WERE HELD TO HONOR HIS ASCENSION.

PERSEUS HIMSELF PARTICIPATED.
WHOOPS!

A STRAY THROW SENT A DISCUS INTO THE CROWD.

WHERE IT STRUCK AND KILLED ACRISIUS, WHO HAD BEEN WATCHING IN DISGUISE.
FATE DOES INDEED WORK IN MYSTERIOUS WAYS.

PERSEUS WOULD BE A GREAT KING, AND HIS CHILDREN WOULD FOUND MANY GREAT NATIONS.
TRUE TO HIS WORD, HE RETURNED THE HEAD OF MEDUSA TO ATHENA.

AT LAST.

NOW...NOW MY AEGIS FEELS COMPLETE.
THEREAFTER, THE AEGIS BECAME ATHENA'S MOST POWERFUL WEAPON, HER MOST SACRED SYMBOL. NATIONS WOULD RISE UP BEHIND IT, AND ARMIES WOULD FLEE IN TERROR AT ITS APPROACH.

THERE REMAINS YET ONE LAST STORY TO RELATE, AND THEN WE ARE DONE.

IN THE COUNTRY OF LYDIA, THERE LIVED A MORTAL WOMAN NAMED ARACHNE. SHE WAS A WEAVER OF UNPARALLELED SKILL.
SHE WOULD SCARCELY EVER TAKE A REST, WORKING DAY AND NIGHT AT HER LOOM, CREATING TAPESTRIES OF EXQUISITE QUALITY.

THE DEMAND FOR THEM WAS GREAT, AND SOON ARACHNE'S FAME HAD SPREAD FAR AND WIDE.
HER TAPESTRIES WERE SO BEAUTIFUL THAT SOME CLAIMED THEY COULD NOT HAVE BEEN MADE WITHOUT DIVINE INTERVENTION.

THE GODS COULD DO NO BETTER
REPLY.

FROM THE CROWD THAT ASSEMBLED DAILY TO WATCH ARACHNE WORK, AN OLD WOMAN ADVISED CAUTION.

BE HUMBLE, MY LADY, AND GIVE THE GODS THEIR DUE. YOUR WORK IS BEAUTIFUL, BUT IT CANNOT MATCH THAT OF LADY ATHENA.
ARACHNE SCOFFED.
IF ATHENA CAN DO BETTER, SHE SHOULD COME DOWN AND PROVE IT.
NEEDLESS TO SAY, SHE GOT HER WISH.

ATHENA AND ARACHNE, THE TWO BACK TO BACK, EACH SPENT THE NIGHT CRAFTING A TAPESTRY OF THEIR OWN DEVISING.
INHUMANLY FAST, THEIR HANDS GLIDED OVER THE STRANDS OF THEIR LOOMS: PULLING, TWISTING, TEASING IMAGES INTO BEING.

THE NEXT DAY, HELIOS'S RAYS WARMED THE LYDIAN COUNTRYSIDE.
OUTSIDE, THE CROWDS ASSEMBLED TO SEE WHAT ATHENA AND ARACHNE HAD CREATED.

ATHENA'S WAS MAGNIFICENT, BEAUTIFUL, DEPICTING HER FATHER'S VICTORY OVER THE TITANS.
IT SEEMED AS IF YOU COULD ALMOST HEAR ZEUS BREATHING. HIS LIGHTNING BOLT SHIMMERED AND SPARKLED LIKE A LIVING THING.

ARACHNE'S WAS EQUALLY BREATHTAKING, BUT ARACHNE'S...

ARACHNE'S TAPESTRY ALSO HAD THE GODS AS THEIR SUBJECT. THOUGH WHERE ATHENA'S CELEBRATED THEM...

ARACHNE'S MOCKED THEM AND MADE FUN OF THEM.

IT SHOWED THEM AS CLOWNS, AS FOOLS.

ARACHNE REALIZED TOO LATE THAT SHE HAD GONE TOO FAR.

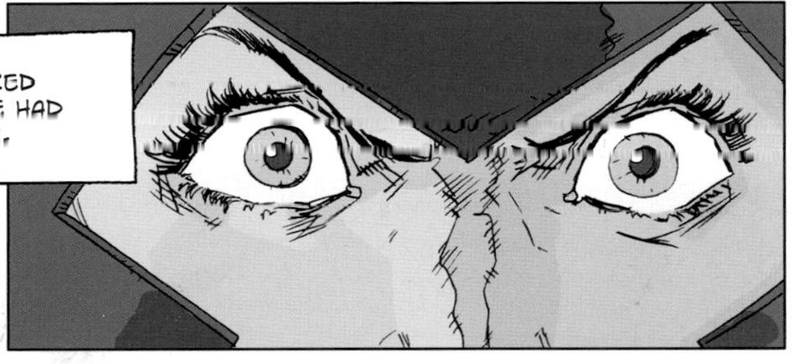

YOU
YOUR WORK IS FLAWLESS.
BUT YOU...

YOU ARE SO **SMALL**.

POOR ARACHNE.
BUT WHAT CAN ONE EXPECT
WHEN ONE TRIFLES WITH THE GODS?

OUR PICTURE OF ATHENA IS NOW COMPLETE.
THERE ARE MANY MORE TALES OF HER TO BE TOLD. ENOUGH TO FILL A THOUSAND WALLS WITH A HUNDRED THOUSAND TAPESTRIES.
BUT WHAT HAS BEEN TOLD WILL SUFFICE FOR NOW.

Where to start? A quick note on the text before I dive into talking about Athena.

The Greek myths are older than the written word. There's no set version of how events occurred. In the ancient days, people had their own local stories of how things came to be, and most times these stories didn't agree. With no single source, these stories were passed down through the ages by bards, who sang of heroes and their deeds. I went as far back to the original sources as I could in my retellings of these myths. As I added my own twists here and there, I made connections that were not so apparent, creating a tapestry of Greek mythology.

The four Greek goddesses we hear the most about are Aphrodite (the goddess of love), Artemis (the goddess of forests, hills, and the hunt), Hera (the goddess of marriage), and Athena (the goddess of war and wisdom).

Sometimes we also hear about Nike, because of the shoes.

Of these four goddesses, Athena has the greatest physical power. Even Athena's birth is violent. How many kids have to start their lives pounding their way out from inside their immortal and invincible father's skull? I only know of the one.

Athena doesn't stop there—this book is filled with stories about her fighting (and overcoming) much bigger, stronger, and older opponents, most of whom happen to be guys. And when Athena's not fighting her own battles, she's offering advice and resources to less powerful people who can do the job for her—presumably because even though she's a goddess, she's nice enough to leave some of the tamer monsters for the humans who like that sort of thing. She's not just strong: she's smart, too.

That's pretty awesome.

Unfortunately, the place of women in the Greek society that worshipped Athena doesn't reflect her position as a super-smart, super-powerful member of the Olympian pantheon.

Greek women couldn't own property, vote, or even chose who they wanted to marry. No adventures for them! They were expected to take care of the kids and the house—that's about it. And though a few women did learn to read and write, they weren't generally thought of as possessing the wisdom that's one of Athena's trademarks (though there were a few poets, priestesses, and oracles who were exceptions to that rule).

I'm glad that I live in a time when girls can be more like Athena—a time when women are breaking athletic records, making scientific discoveries, and on the whole, succeeding in ways they've never been allowed to before. Ladies, you rock.

George O'Connor
Brooklyn, NY
2009

A BRIEF NOTE ON NAMES

Some readers may notice that the names of some of the characters in Olympians are spelled differently than they may have learned—for example Ouranos instead of Uranus, or Kronos instead of Cronus. This is because, whenever possible, I have tried to use the more "Greek" transliterations of their names, rather than the more familiar Latinized versions.

GODDESS OF Wisdom, War (the beneficial side of it), Strategy, Crafts, Cities
ROMAN NAME Minerva
SYMBOLS Helmet, Spear, Shield, Aegis
SACRED ANIMAL Owl
SACRED PLANT Olive
SACRED PLACES Athens, Greece (her patron city), Libya (site of her training with Pallas), Mount Olympus (home of the Olympian gods)
PLANET Pallas, an asteroid in orbit between Mars and Jupiter.
MODERN LEGACY The modern capital of Greece, Athens, is named after Athena. One of the most famous and enduring symbols of Western civilization is the Parthenon, a temple complex built atop a hill overlooking Athens.
ATHENA
GREY-EYED GODDESS

PAGES 2-3: A brief recap of the events of OLYMPIANS BOOK 1, ZEUS: KING OF THE GODS

PAGES 2-3, PANEL 1: "Moirae" translates directly as "shares" or "portions," and refers to the life that each person is allotted by the Fates.

PAGE 5, PANEL 2: Metis's name in Greek means "counsel"—accordingly, she's the goddess of good advice.

PAGE 5, PANELS 3, 4: The other "distraction" mentioned is Hera, future queen of the gods, pictured walking here with her sister Demeter. Much, much more on Hera in OLYMPIANS BOOK 3, THE GLORY OF HERA.

PAGE 11: We meet the sons of Zeus and Hera here: Ares, the god of war, and Hephaistos, the god of fire and metalworking.

PAGE 13, PANEL 2: Klothos, one of the Fates, has a name that translates as "Spinner." She's often depicted holding a spindle of thread, the thread of life.

PAGE 13, PANEL 3: While they were both gods of war, Athena was the goddess of skill and strategy, whereas Ares was the god of bloodlust and savagery.

PAGE 13, PANEL 4: Likewise, while both were gods of crafts, Hephaistos was the god of the noisy and sooty forge, whereas Athena was the goddess of the refined weaving loom.

PAGE 13 PANEL 4: As a virgin goddess, Athena had no interest in children. The child Demeter is holding is her daughter, Kore, or Persephone. Much more on her in OLYMPIANS BOOK 4, HADES: THE WEALTHY ONE.

PAGE 16, PANEL 3: Pallas means "spear-brandishing." The ancient Greeks also sometimes reckoned that Athena was called Pallas Athena because she was born from Zeus's head holding a spear.

PAGE 17, PANEL 7: Athena is reflecting on why she feels unwelcome on Olympus. Zeus's family understandably viewed the arrival of this new goddess, who was apparently born entirely clothed from the head of Zeus, with distrust. In fact, according to some traditions, Hera gave birth to Hephaistos herself, with no involvement from Zeus at all, in order to counter Zeus's "birth" of Athena. She did this by eating lettuce and smacking the ground with the flat of her palm. Now you know why I didn't include this version. ;)

PAGE 19: There were no contests of wrestling, though—Heracles hadn't invented it yet.

PAGE 25, PANEL 1: Lakhesis means "dispenser of lots." She was the Fate who measured out the allotted life span of every living thing.

PAGE 27: THE GIGANTES, from whom we get the modern words giant and gigantic, translate directly as "born from the Earth." As I've deliberately conflated the Furies with the Fates (see ZEUS: KING OF THE GODS), the Fates are sisters to the Gigantes: all were born from the drops of Ouranos's blood that the Titan Kronos spilled on the Earth.

PAGES 28-29: An assemblage of twelve Olympians (though not necessarily the final twelve).
CLOCKWISE FROM TOP LEFT ARE: Demeter, Hera, Zeus, Aphrodite, Poseidon, Hermes, Hephaistos, Athena, Ares, Apollo, Artemis, and Hestia.

PAGE 32, PANEL 5: Poor Ares. This is why it pays to think, kids. Luckily, as he was the immortal god of war, only his pride was hurt.

PAGE 34: Obviously a different Pallas from the one we met before. In some sources, Pallas is a Titan, and not a Gigante—however, Titans are immortal, so it seems unlikely Athena would have been able to skin him. He's Titan-sized, though, that's for sure.

PAGE 39, PANEL 2: Watch future volumes for more on Mother Earth's attempts to dethrone Zeus.

PAGE 40: The name Medusa means "Queen" or "Guardian."

PAGE 42, PANEL 1: Danae was thought of as the ancestor of the Danaan people, a name often applied to all of the Greeks.

PAGE 43, PANEL 3: Perseus is thought to mean "the Destroyer." He certainly does create a lot of damage throughout this story.

PAGE 45, PANEL 2: Hermes and Athena, the favorite, and most trustworthy of Zeus' s children, were often partnered to help heroes on their quests. You'll definitely be seeing this pairing again.

PAGE 46, PANEL 5: A tale for another day...

PAGE 46, PANEL 6: Perseus asks for a helmet of invisibility because in some versions he is lent the invisibility-granting helmet of Hades. I opted to leave this out because, really, he has enough help already. Make him work for it a little! Even I could kill Medusa if I could turn invisible too.

PAGE 46, PANEL 7: In some sources the Graeae are sisters of Medusa and the Gorgons. The motif of three goddesses in ancient Greece was very popular; for example, with the Fates, the Furies, the Graeae, and the Gorgons are all comprised of three goddesses.

PAGE 55: Pegasus, the famous winged horse, was the child of Medusa and Poseidon (the god of horses, among other things). He was born when Perseus cut off Medusa's head.

PAGE 56: The Gorgons (terrible, fierce) were the immortal sisters of Medusa. They were Euryale (wide-stepping) and Sthenno (strength). Medusa was the third Gorgon. Myth does not record what they did to so anger Athena.

PAGE 57, PANEL 3: This sea monster's name, "Cetus," means "whale." The scientific name for whales is Cetacean, after this beast.

PAGE 60, PANEL 5: He's not called the Destroyer for nothing, folks.

PAGE 61: Remember kids: never mess with Athena.

PAGE 62, PANEL 5: The myths depicted in Arachne's tapestries are, from left to right, the birth of Aphrodite from sea foam, the escape of Daedalus and Icarus from the Labyrinth, and the battle of the Centaurs and Lapiths

PAGE 65: The myths Arachne depicted are: PANEL 1: Zeus and Europa; PANEL 2: Zeus and Leda; PANEL 3: Athena's slaying of her friend Pallas; PANEL 4: Zeus's swallowing of Metis

PAGE 66: What the—? Didn't Arachne read the note for page 61? Arachne means "spider," and the scientific name for spiders is Arachnid. Arachnophobia is the term for the fear of spiders.

PERSEUS

THE FIRST OF THE HEROES

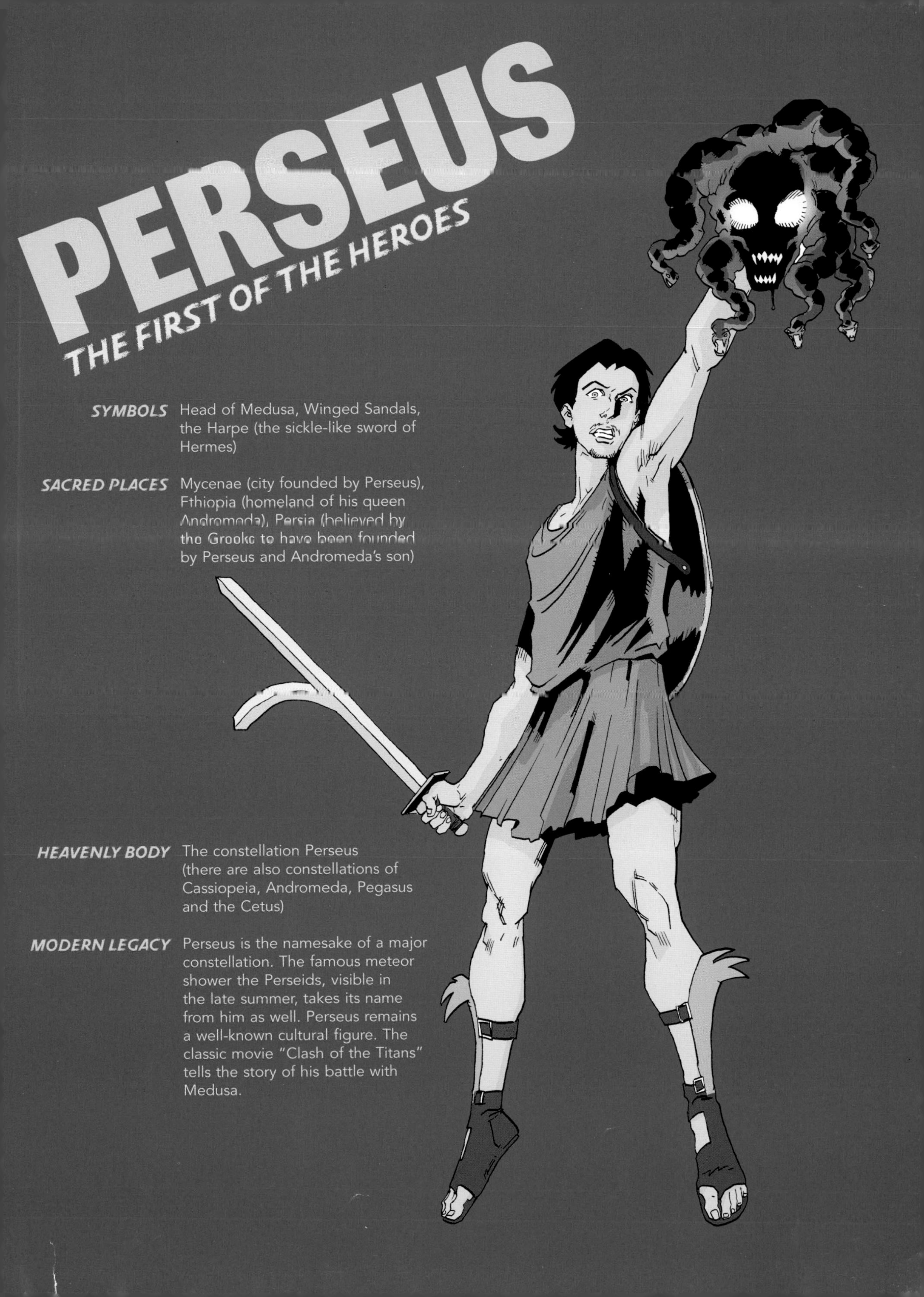

SYMBOLS Head of Medusa, Winged Sandals, the Harpe (the sickle-like sword of Hermes)

SACRED PLACES Mycenae (city founded by Perseus), Ethiopia (homeland of his queen Andromeda), Persia (believed by the Greeks to have been founded by Perseus and Andromeda's son)

HEAVENLY BODY The constellation Perseus (there are also constellations of Cassiopeia, Andromeda, Pegasus and the Cetus)

MODERN LEGACY Perseus is the namesake of a major constellation. The famous meteor shower the Perseids, visible in the late summer, takes its name from him as well. Perseus remains a well-known cultural figure. The classic movie "Clash of the Titans" tells the story of his battle with Medusa.

ABOUT THIS BOOK

ATHENA: GREY-EYED GODDESS is the second book in OLYMPIANS, a new graphic novel series from First Second that retells the Greek myths. This is the story of one of the most powerful of the Greek goddesses, Athena. She is the goddess of wisdom, peace, warfare, strategy, handcrafts, and reason.

FOR DISCUSSION

1. Perseus had to have a lot of courage to hunt down Medusa. What's the bravest thing you've ever done or ever seen someone else do?

2. A lot of the names in this book will sound familiar; for example, Titan and Arachne. What other things can you think of that have names similar to characters in Greek mythology?

3. The gods and goddesses in this book have powers like changing shape, throwing lightning bolts, and foretelling the future. Which of these powers seems like the best? Which would you most like to have? Is the answer to those two questions the same?

4. In many ways, Athena and the other characters are like superheroes. What superheroes can you think of that are similar to the characters in Greek mythology?

5. Athena's story is narrated by the three Fates, who can see the future. They know everything before it happens. If the Fates know everything that happens in the future, does Athena still have to act to bring the future about? What happens if she sits and does nothing?

6. In the story of Arachne, Athena deals with her anger at Arachne by turning her into a spider. Is this a good way to deal with conflict? Are there better animals to turn Arachne into?

7. Very few people believe in the Greek gods today. Why do you think it is important that we learn about them?

NAME TRANSLATION "Queen"

HER SISTERS Euryale ("Wide-Stepping") and Stheno ("Strong")

SYMBOL Medusa's own head, called a gorgoneion, was widely used in the ancient world as a protection for homes and temples. It can still be seen many places today.

HEAVENLY BODY In addition to her severed head being part of the constellation Perseus, Medusa has her own nebula (a giant space-cloud of gas and dust) that was discovered in modern times.

MODERN LEGACY The word for jellyfish in Spanish is medusa. It's not that hard to see the resemblance!

MEDUSA

THE GORGON

BIBLIOGRAPHY

***HESIOD: VOLUME 1, THEOGENY. WORKS AND DAYS: TESTIMONIA.* HESIOD. NEW YORK: LOEB CLASSICAL LIBRARY, 2007.**
The above is the copy I have in my personal collection; it was the best translation I found.

***THEOI GREEK MYTHOLOGY WEB SITE.* WWW.THEOI.COM**
Without a doubt, the single most valuable resource I came across in this entire venture. At theoi.com, you can find an encyclopedia of various gods and goddesses from Greek mythology, cross referenced with every mention of them found in literally hundreds of ancient Greek and Roman texts.

***METAMORPHOSES.* OVID. NEW YORK: PENGUIN CLASSICS, 2004.**
An excellent translation. Although Ovid was actually Roman (and Athena goes by her Roman name Minerva here), his is the only account we have of the story of Arachne (though the story does appear to be pictured on some Greek vases).

***MYTH INDEX WEB SITE* WWW.MYTHINDEX.COM**
It seems this Web site is connected in some way to Theoi.com, and is still being updated, which is nice. While it doesn't have the painstakingly compiled quotations of ancient texts, it does offer some terrific encyclopedic entries about virtually every character ever to pass through a Greek myth. Pretty amazing.

ALSO RECOMMENDED

FOR YOUNGER READERS

The Gods and Goddesses of Olympus. Aliki. New York: HarperCollins, 1997.

D'Aulaires' Book of Greek Myths. Ingri and Edgar Parin D'Aulaire. New York: Doubleday, 1962.

Black Ships Before Troy. Rosemary Sutcliff and Alan Lee. London: Francis Lincoln, 2005.

Wanderings of Odysseus. Rosemary Sutcliff and Alan Lee. London: Francis Lincoln, 2005.

We Goddesses: Athena, Aphrodite, Hera. Doris Orgel, illustrated by Marilee Heyer. New York: DK Publishing, 1999.

Z Is for Zeus: A Greek Mythology Alphabet. Helen L. Wilbur and Victor Juhasz. Chelsea MI: Sleeping Bear Press, 2008.

FOR OLDER READERS

Athena: A Biography. Lee Hall. Reading MA: Perseus Publishing, 1997.

The Marriage of Cadmus and Harmony. Robert Calasso. New York: Knopf, 1993.

Mythology. Edith Hamilton. New York: Grand Central Publishing, 1999.

The MOIRAE

SPINNERS OF FATE

GODDESSES OF Fate, the inescapable destiny of men and women

INDIVIDUAL NAMES Klotho ("The Spinner"), Lakhesis ("The Dispenser of Lots"), Atropos ("Cannot Be Turned")

ROMAN NAMES (as a group) the Parcae, the Fatae (individually) Nona, Decuma, and Morta

SYMBOLS Spindle, Thread, Loom, Scissors

SACRED ANIMAL Dove

SACRED PLACES Corinth, Olympia, Thebes, Sparta (sites for their worship in ancient Greece)

MODERN LEGACY Our own word "fate," which is derived from one of the Latin names for these goddesses; people still occasionally say "if the Fates allow."

To Steve. We all miss you.
– G.O.

New York & London

A Neal Porter Book
Published by First Second
First Second is an imprint of Roaring Brook Press,
a division of Holtzbrinck Publishing Holdings Limited Partnership
175 Fifth Avenue, New York, New York 10010

Distributed in the United Kingdom by Macmillan Children's Books,
a division of Pan Macmillan.

Cataloging-in-Publication Data is on file at the Library of Congress

Paperback ISBN: 978-1-59643-432-5
Hardcover ISBN: 978-1-59643-649-7

First Edition April 2010

Cover design by Mark Siegel and Colleen AF Venable
Book design by Colleen AF Venable and Danica Novgorodoff

Printed in China by Toppan Leefung Printing Ltd., Dongguan City, Guangdong Province.

Paperback: 20 19 18 17 16 15 14 13 12 11
Hardcover: 10 9 8 7